Foreword

I remember first meeting Cyndi. She was full of energy and excitement, but there was something different about her that I couldn't put my finger on.

Once I got to know Cyndi a little better, I found out what that "something" was. You see, Cyndi spent most of her working life as an accomplished paramedic. She has seen and experienced things that I can only imagine.

The stories she tells from her previous career are full of excitement and passion for the people and patients she served. "Something" was really a combination of great traits. Cyndi is smart, gritty, determined, vocal, and compassionate (an uncommon combination).

She cares more about her clients' well-being than she does about her own—just like she did as a paramedic. I have been lucky enough to get to know and work with Cyndi. If you get the chance, you should too.

Max Robinson
Gateway Mortgage Group Area Manager
704-490-2774
max.robertson@gatewayloan.com

© Copyright 2018 Cyndi Griffin.

Table Of Contents

Buying a home is exciting and rewarding but it can be frightening as well. There have been many recent changes to lending laws and the process of buying a home in North Carolina. Whether you are a first-time buyer, looking for a larger home to fit your growing family or downsizing, the information in these pages will give you an overview of what to expect on your homeownership journey.

Page	Section
7	Why Buy?
9	Find A Realtor
11	Pre-Qualification
13	Searching For A Home
15	How Much Money Do I Need?
17	Down Payment
19	Closing Costs
21	Due Diligence Period
23	Due Diligence Fee
25	Earnest Money
27	Home Inspection
29	Survey
31	Appraisal
33	Minimum Cash Needed
35	Closing
36	About The Author

Why Buy?

- **Predictable Monthly Housing Payments**

  Bonus! Your payments go toward your homeownership, not your landlord's.

- **Appreciation**

  You'll have an asset that will most likely increase in value over time.

- **Tax Benefits**

  Many expenses of owning a home are tax deductible.

- **It's Cheaper!**

  It is still cheaper to buy than rent in the majority of US markets. Plus, interest rates are still at historic lows.

- **Built In Rainy Day Fund**

  Homeownership provides you with the opportunity to borrow money on the equity you eventually build up by consistently paying your mortgage.

- **It's Yours!**

  With a rental, you can get kicked out at the end of your lease.

Find A Realtor

This is the first step. You need someone who represents you and is legally bound to protect your interests. You will need to sign a Buyer's Agency Agreement. This not a contract and can be rescinded any time but is it a legal document that binds the realtor to you and gives them the responsibility of placing your needs above all others, including their own.

A licensed Broker/Realtor will see that you get the best deal possible and will take care of the negotiations and the vast amount of paperwork involved.

Pre-Qualification

A pre-qualification states that you are an excellent candidate for a home loan. This is based on your income, debt and credit score. It isn't a guarantee of acceptance but rather an indicator that you should be able to gain a loan approval.

Talk to a reputable lender to obtain this very important document. You will need it to place an offer on a home. Your Realtor works with lenders on a regular basis and has forged professional relationships with those that they trust. Listen to their advice. He or she can guide you in this crucial choice.

Searching For A Home

Your Realtor will help you through this process. Heed their advice when choosing. Online home search websites are a good place to get ideas but your Realtor has access to more homes and have information and updates not available to you online.

They have the experience to spot pitfalls and to guide you to a home that fits your wants and needs.

How Much Money Do I Need?

This depends on a lot of factors. The price of the home, the type of loan you obtain and the services you order during the home buying process.

Following are some estimates of what you will need to have on hand to purchase your new home.

Please note that all estimates are for illustrative purposes only and are subject to change.

Down Payment

This depends on your mortgage and your situation. Typically, it can be anywhere between 0% (no down payment) and 20% of the sale price of the home.

Down payment assistance may be available to you. These programs have specific qualifications that the buyer and the home being purchased must meet. Some loans, like VA and USDA, may cover the entire amount. Be sure to discuss these with your lender.

Closing Costs

These are costs paid at closing. They cover the costs of the loan, attorney fees, insurance and taxes to name a few.

The amount varies from home purchase to home purchase. Sometimes it can be negotiated that the seller pays part or all of the buyer's closing costs. If a high enough sale price is offered it may be incentive for the seller to assist the buyer with this expense.

Some down payment assistance programs can be used to cover some or all of the closing costs.

Talk to your Realtor and Lender about this.

Due Diligence Period

This is a period that begins the day you go under contract to buy your new home. This occurs when both the buyer and the seller agree on the terms of purchase and both have signed the offer. When that happens, the offer then becomes the contract. The duration of the Due Diligence period is negotiable and is stated in the contract.

This is a time for you and your Realtor to investigate the home to make sure that you indeed want to complete the purchase. You may want to obtain a home inspection and survey to help you make this decision. Your Realtor can assist you in these decisions and make recommendations for providers of these services and order them for you.

If, during Due Diligence, you find that the home you have contracted to buy does not meet your needs you can terminate the contract for "any or no reason".

Due Diligence Fee

The Due Diligence Fee is money paid directly to the seller to compensate them for keeping the home off the market during the Due Diligence Period.

The amount is negotiable. For a home priced between $100,000 and $300,000, common due diligence fees range between $200 and $1500. If there is more than one offer on a home, a higher Due Diligence Fee could be incentive for the seller to choose your offer.

The Due Diligence fee is credited toward the sale price of the home at closing. **If you decide not to buy the home the seller will keep this money.**

Earnest Money

Earnest Money is paid prior to closing as a "good faith" gesture to the seller to show that you are serious about buying their home. It too is negotiable but will usually fall between $200 and $1500 for the price range of $100,000 and $300,000. Of course, it can be higher or lower depending on the agreement between the buyer and seller. It is made payable to the holder of the escrow account for your transaction. This could be the real estate firm, the closing attorney or a title company.

It is held in the escrow account and the amount is credited toward the sale price at closing. If you decide not to buy during the Due Diligence Period, the Earnest Money Deposit will be returned to you. If you make that decision after the Due Diligence Period ends, it will go to the seller.

Home Inspection

It is recommended that you obtain a home inspection to discover the condition of the home you are purchasing.

There are several types to choose from. A general, comprehensive inspection is advised as is a termite inspection. Some types of mortgages will require one or both of these.

The cost of inspections can run from $400 to $1000 (and sometimes higher depending on the size of the home).

You can usually have this cost deferred to closing and rolled into the closing costs. If you decide to not buy the home you will be still be responsible for the inspection fee.

Survey

It is recommended that you get a survey during the Due Diligence Period.

Many headaches can be averted down the road when you know your exact property boundaries. A survey will also discover any problems with those boundaries such as easements and intrusions that may not be noticeable with the naked eye.

This can run between $400 and $1500 depending on the size of your lot. It could be higher if there is acreage involved. You can usually have this cost deferred to closing and rolled into the closing costs. If you decide to not buy the home you will still be responsible for this survey fee.

Appraisal

Your lender will order an appraisal. This is an independent, third party determination of the market value of the home that you are purchasing.

This almost always has to be paid upfront. Appraisal costs average $400 to $800+ depending on the size and location of the home.

This is a very important step in the home buying process because it will determine the amount the mortgage company will loan you on a given home. Your Realtor will study recent sales in the vicinity of your home that are comparable in size, quality and condition to determine an offer price that should appraise.

Just another reason to have a reputable Realtor on your side!

Minimum Cash Needed

So! Here we are at the original question!

Based on the items we have discussed, and not including a down payment (if required), a person buying a home in North Carolina with a price between $100,000 and $300,000 will need in the range of $1,600 - $6,300 *(this is an estimate)*.

Some of this will be credited at closing but it is necessary to have the funds upfront to facilitate the sale. Your Realtor and your Lender will advise you of what you will need based on your income, interest rate and the price point of the home you are seeking.

Closing

Hopefully this little booklet has given you the information you need to embark on the exciting and rewarding journey to home ownership. If there are any questions that were not answered in these pages please do not hesitate to contact me. I would be honored to assist you any way I can. My contact information is on the next page.

Good luck and Happy House Hunting!!!

About the Author

Cyndi Griffin is a residential real estate Broker/REALTOR in North Carolina. Though she works with clients in all buyer and seller situations, she enjoys focusing on first time homebuyers and downsizers. She also works with active duty military and veterans for which she holds the Military Residential Specialist certification.

She spent many years as a Paramedic Crew-Chief in Charlotte, NC and brings the same level of customer service and support to her real estate clients as she did her patients in her EMS career. She places their needs before all others including her own.

Cyndi has three children and nine grandchildren and lives with her husband Jeff in Albemarle, NC.

www.ingramcontent.com/pod-product-compliance
Lightning Source LLC
Chambersburg PA
CBHW040255220526
45473CB00001B/494